THE STAGES OF CHILD DEVELOPMENT

By

DR HELEN ALLEY

Table Of Contents

Introduction

Chapter 1: Arrangement With The Specialist

- The Part Of The Eager Father

- Physical Preparation Of The Mother

- Mental Arrangement Of The Mother

- Fantasies Connected With Pregnancy

- Inconveniences Of Pregnancy

- Equipment Of The New Child

Chapter 2: The Child Arrival

- Carriers Of Heredity

- Boy Or Girl

- Multiple Births

- Conduct Of The Infant

- The Child In The Family

Chapter 3: Physical Development Of The Child

- Relation Of Physical Development To Mental Development

- Height And Weight

- Body Proportions

- Significance Of Body Proportions

- The Baby's Bones

- The Baby's Teeth

- Illness In Babyhood

- What To Do About Crying

Chapter 4: Emotional And Social Development

- Introduction

- What Is Personality?

- Factors Influencing Emotional And Social
  Development

Chapter 5: Intellectual Development

- The Brain And Its Capabilities

- How A Child Learns

Chapter 6: Children Sickness

- Hospitalization Of Children

- Mental Effects Of Illness

- Common Physical Defects

Chapter 7: Childhood Accidents

Chapter 8: Acquiring Skills

- Childhood The Brilliant Age To Acquire Skills

- Essentials In Acquiring Skills

- Speech Skills

- Understanding What Others Say

- Aids In Understanding

- What Amount Does A Child Fathom?

- Social Values Of Speech

Chapter 9: The Child's Responsibility

- Responsibilities Regarding His Space

- Responsibilities In The Home.

- Psychological Values Of Home Responsibilities

Chapter 10: Discipline-good And Bad

- Components Of Discipline

- Kinds Of Discipline

- Teaching For Discipline

- Alerts In Teaching For Discipline

- Great Instructive Practices In Discipline

- Award For Good Way Of Behaving

- Discipline For Bad Conduct

- Unacceptable Types Of Discipline.

- Great Types Of Discipline

Chapter 11: School Kickoff

- Importance Of Early School Experiences

- Going To School - An Adjustment

- Emotional Tension Accompanying Adjustment.

- Preliminary Adjustments Are Helpful.

- Significant Areas Of Adjustment

INTRODUCTION

Have you here and there invited another child into your family bunch? On the off chance that you view it as quite possibly the most earth shattering occasion in your everyday life. An expansion to the family brings extreme and super durable changes. Child's coming will fairly change the existence of each and every one in the gathering and shrewd and mature guardians will understand that all individuals should be mentally prepared.Ideally all groundwork for another child (material, physical and mental) ought to start when the specialist illuminates the lady that she is pregnant. Mental arrangement is frequently than not a higher priority than actual planning in view of its drawn out impact on the mother's relationship with her kid. Planning for the child's appearance not just make it workable for her to be prepared in front of time,but considerably more significant, it takes out the exhausted and turmoil brought about by last minutes readiness ;likewise early readiness assists the mother with adapting to the issues of really focusing on an infant with serenity and fearlessness - characteristics that are so fundamental for the child's acclimation to his new life outside the mother's body.

Chapter 1

Arrangement with the specialist

When a lady suspects she is pregnant, she ought to go to her primary care physician or a pre-birth facility. She could likewise call a medical clinic and request to have a specialist suggested.

At the point when the specialist's assessment and tests demonstrate that she is pregnant, the lady ought to examine with him useful issues, for example, how long he will believe she should remain in the medical clinic, what kind of room-private, semi private, or ward-she believes she can manage, and what his expense will be. She ought to likewise illuminate him assuming she conveys medical clinic protection.

The specialist, thus, will exhort her about diet, work out, care of teeth during pregnancy, the taking of nutrient and calcium pills, and the amount she might do. He will advise her regarding what she might anticipate that in respect should putting on weight, conceivable morning affliction, fussy hunger, and exhaustion. Many specialists give their patients printed directions. Elucidating leaflets can likewise be gotten from a local area wellbeing administration. The specialist will set ordinary times for occasional tests during pregnancy and recommend that she reach out to him. Would it be a good idea for her if she wants his recommendation between the customary visits.

Most issues going before or going with labor can be met effectively in the event that the lady places herself under the watchful eye of a specialist or pre-birth center when she thinks she is pregnant. More significant still is that she adheres to his directions precisely, despite the fact that they are not the same as those given to her mom, or companions, or to those showing up in papers, magazines, and books. Never, for any reason, would it be a good idea for her to take any medication, even ibuprofen for a migraine, or a purgative for clogging, without first counseling her PCP. Since the thalidomide alarm of 1962, the clinical calling has been asking pregnant ladies to try not to utilize any medications besides with the assent of their primary care physicians.

The Part Of The Eager Father

The dad job in the family is quick losing its conventional spot at home, as sole top of the family, seldom taking an interest besides as a regulation provider, ref, and weighty taskmaster; in any case, in its place, he takes a more dynamic and fulfilling part in the direction and care of the youngsters. His capability is considerably more than that of the provider, out on the planet, fundamentally providing essential actual necessities. To have his cutting edge impact, he is keen on child's government assistance in any event, during pregnancy, and many specialists demand that the spouse go with the wife on a portion of her pre-birth visits.

The eager dad's impact on his better half's physical and mental prosperity is a higher priority than frequently recognized. Support and understanding from him will give her a sense of safety and certainty that no other person can give.

Glandular changes in the mother. to-be now and again produce states of mind or discouragements, from blissful positive feelings to miserable dejection. As a body promotion. just, these miseries vanish. Indeed, even the most calm lady might be irritated with time. An insightful spouse will comprehend and give an exceptional expression of appreciation. He might need to console her that she is as yet appealing and beguiling even without her thin figure. He will show an interest in her eating regimen, her looks, and her rest.

Right now, however they have previously shared issues together, a chivalrous spouse will keep superfluous concern from his significant other. He will understand that she really wants redirections and see that she doesn't pass up great times. Seeing family members and companions, taking part in games or comparative exercises, taking strolls, or perusing together, will be particularly significant assuming that he recommends them and enters these exercises energetically.

His help with family undertakings and doing all truly difficult work and moving will mean as much for her soul concerning her actual prosperity. The tomfoolery and friendship in sharing kitchen obligations will be unwinding for both and improve the sensation of closeness fully expecting the child's coming. Father will likewise find that family abilities procured here may later demonstrate accommodating in the event of mother's ailment or when the child needs extraordinary consideration.

Physical Preparation Of The Mother

The newborn child is totally subject to the mother for sustenance and insurance during the prior month's birth. Hence, it is fundamental that the climate in which the child creates be just about as great as could really be expected. Indeed, even with the best clinical consideration, the obligation regarding keeping an ideal climate rests completely in the possession of the mother.

The sustenance the child gets before his introduction to the world comes from the retention of nutritive items from the mother's circulation system. Her blood, thus, is impacted by her overall ailment and her eating routine. Before, the amount of food eaten by the mother was underlined as significant. Today we realize that it is the nature of the food in the eating regimen that matters. At the end of the day, not how much a mother eats is significant yet what sort of food.

The day to day diet most generally supported today for hopeful moms ought to incorporate food sources recorded in the diagram underneath.

Many specialists today prescribe that when the mother-to-be feels cravings for food between dinners she takes unsweetened gelatin in natural product juice or a gelatin case. This ought not be finished, be that as it may, without the specialist's information and assent. Rich food sources that are vigorously prepared, baked goods, desserts, seared food sources, and greasy meats ought to be kept away from.

A hankering for specific food sources or surprising blends of food sources is genuinely normal, particularly during the early piece of pregnancy. These desires as a rule are created when the eating regimen isn't as expected adjusted. Assuming the hopeful mother permits herself to be directed by these desires, she might eat excessively not many of the food varieties crucial for her child's prosperity. Should the desire for serious areas of strength be steady, the specialist ought to be counseled.

Least day to day food fundamentals for the hopeful lady.

- one quart of milk (entire or skim, as endorsed by specialist)
- One egg
- One serving of lean meat, fish or fowl
- Nutrient and calcium tablets (as recommended by specialist)
- New natural products (no less than two oranges or tangerines)

- Three cuts of buttered entire wheat or improved cereal
- One serving of entire grain or advanced oat
- One cooked and one crude leaf or stem vegetable, like spinach, cabbage, celery, lettuce or asparagus.

Mental Arrangement Of The Mother

The best mental groundwork for a mother is in persuading her that all will work out positively, given she adheres to her PCP's guidance cautiously. Confusions or passing are extremely uncommon in labor today, besides in situations where there has been no clinical consideration or where clinical counsel has been disregarded. Pregnancy is an ordinary, solid condition. On the off chance that the lady can accomplish and keep up with this perspective. Her mental planning will be amazing.

There are regularly when the mother-to-be won't feel like standard, particularly during the early long stretches of pregnancy when morning ailment is normal and in the last option part of pregnancy, when the extra weight and size of the child cause her to feel abnormal, awkward, and tired. Acknowledgment of this as a transitory condition and help from the specialist in limiting these circumstances will go quite far toward working on her demeanor.

Most moms-to-be have a psychological image of what they maintain that the child should be their fantasy youngster. Ordinarily, they understand what sex they need, what they maintain that the youngster should resemble, what capacities they maintain that the kid should have, and what kind of character he will be supplied with. Regularly, the fantasy youngster is the polar opposite of what the parent is. On the off chance that, for instance, the lady feels that her victories, scholastically and socially, were underneath what she maintained that they should be, she might fantasize about having a kid whose looks, knowledge, and character make the person in question a star in each circle of life.

One of the most troublesome, but generally significant, parts of the mother's mental readiness is

to settle on a choice to acknowledge her youngster
as he is. Since the child will acquire physical and
mental qualities like those of his folks, needing a
child with qualities that are the polar opposite of his
folks' is a vain expectation.

A sluggish, continuous acknowledgment of the
obligations and penances of parenthood will go far
to help a youthful mother-to-be set herself up
mentally for the appearance of her child.
Consistently she could tell herself, "How might I
deal with my work and entertainment today on the
off chance that I had a child?" she ought to sort out
intellectually a strategy that would be functional
with a child in the home.
Mental planning ought not be restricted to the
principal child. The mother-to-be should prepare
herself intellectually to acknowledge any new child
into her life, while simultaneously keeping away
from any disturbance of the relationship that exists
among herself and her significant other and different
kids. Besides, she should understand that another
child will add new work and new obligations.
Similarly, she should understand that there will be
friction and desire toward the new child with respect
to different youngsters, despite the fact that they

guarantee they can "barely hold back to see the new conceived child".

Fantasies Connected With Pregnancy

No part of medication is more hampered by customs from the past than is what manages the pregnancy time frame. Youthful moms-to-be are cautioned by good natured family members and companions that assuming they do either it will meaningfully affect the children creating inside their bodies. For instance, that's what certain individuals trust assuming a mother revels in strawberries or beverages wine the child will have strawberry checks or wine blotches on his skin.

Since there is no association between the sensory systems of the mother and her child, the mother'scontemplations can't significantly affect her child. Nonetheless, as the child retains water, oxygen, and nutritive items from the mother's blood, an unfortunate state of her blood will influence the child in relation to the seriousness of the condition that exists.

There is a broadly held conventional conviction that rashly conceived infants are ill-fated to a physical and mental soft spot until the end of their lives. Except if there has been a harm to the child's mind upon entering the world, there is no proof at all that pre-development will affect the child's improvement other than to dial it back to some degree during the principal little while of life.

Acknowledgment of the conviction that rashly conceived infants are ill-fated to be physical and mental quitters makes many guardians be overprotective. Thus, they Heprive the child ofchildof the chances to do what he can do, and this makes him be genuinely and intellectually in reverse for his age. Far and away more terrible, it makes him uncertain of himself, and this urges him to be reliant long after he is fit for being autonomous.

Then there is a deception about the connection between the time a child is conceived and his physical and intellectual abilities. The old nursery rhyme about `Mon day's child is fair of face,

Tuesday's youngster is brimming with elegance," underlines the conviction about a connection between the kid's capacities and the day of the week on which he was conceived. There is positively no logical proof to validate such convictions, and there is a lot of proof to refute them.

The significant thing about old spouses' stories is that many individuals acknowledge them in a careless manner and, far more terrible, act as per these convictions, in any event, when they are in direct inconsistency to present day clinical information. A mother-to-be, for instance, may have been encouraged by her primary care physician to chop down her food admission to elim inate the chance of her child's turning out to be huge to the point that it would create problems at the hour of birth. In any case, assuming that she had forever been informed that a mother-to-be should cat for two, she could overlook the counsel of her PCP, subsequently imperiling her own life as well as that of her child too.

Inconveniences Of Pregnancy

Prior to passing on the conversation of the mother's wellbeing to perceive how "child" is doing, referencing the absolute most incessant difficulties of pregnancy would be well. A few ladies go through a whole pregnancy with no; others report being somewhat irritated by a few. The specialist will be glad to examine them and reduce fears. Generally normal among gentle inconveniences is morning sickness. To combat this, the basic strategy of keeping soft drink wafers at the bedside to eat prior to lifting the head from the cushion in the first part of the day functions admirably. Serious and drawn out queasiness ought to be accounted for to the specialist. Numerous successful drugs are accessible. Indigestion is a stomach related unsettling influence not exactly connected with the heart. Windedness brought about by the expanding uterus squeezing upwards against the lungs. Varicose veins create from unfortunate course because of tension and squeezing of veins. Rest, with raised legs and feet as recently referenced, gives help. The utilization of elasticized stockings and explicit activities likewise helps. Muscle cramps in - the legs are feeling better by rest. Drugs are additionally accessible.

While these milder entanglements might be examined at the following specialist's meeting, serious side effects ought to be accounted for on the double. They might be trailblazers of risky complexities. Among these side effects are enlargement of face and hands, obscured vision, draining from the vagina, fever, tipsiness, or stomach torments. On the off chance that any of these happen, the mother ought to hit the hay in the wake of calling her PCP. Many compromised unnatural birth cycles have been ended with legitimate clinical management.

Luckily, the unfavorable impacts of German Measles have been found. The mother's doctor will prompt every such risk.

Equipment Of The New Child

One misstep that youthful guardians frequently make is to secure more gear for the principal child than is totally needed. They neglect to perceive that a child stays little for an exceptionally brief time frame and consequently grows out of baby hardware very soon. Additionally frequently ignored is the way that they will get a few hardware as gifts and offer the utilization of some gear borrowed from family members or companions.

On account of a first child, it is very normal for family members and companions to give child showers with gifts for the new child. At the point when the mother-to-be is asked what she wants, she can constantly recommend things that will be fundamental when the child is first conceived or when he is more seasoned. A preparation latrine for instance, is a need before the child is a year old but a couple of individuals would consider giving it a gift except if the mother-to-be proposed it. Assuming

there are copies, they can be traded for gear
expected to fill in holes of basics.

Chapter 2

The Child Arrival

Life starts at the hour of origination which is around nine months before birth. While this might appear to be a brief time frame corresponding to the life expectancy of the individual, it is essentially significant in figuring out what the singular will be. When his birthday shows up, a child is now a particular and achieved individual by his own doing. He is 280 days old and he has expanded his weight multiple times.

Carriers Of Heredity

Inside the sex cells of each and every man and lady are 23 sets of chromo somes. A chromosome is a threadlike molecule which contains strings of moment particles called "qualities." The qualities are the genuine transporters of heredity since they are the actual substances given from parent to youngster. The guardians' qualities, thus, have come from their folks and grandparents, and so on.

It has been assessed that there are somewhere in the range of 80,000 and 120,000 qualities in each sex cell. A portion of the qualities are liable for deciding actual qualities, for example, level, hair tone, or size and state of nose, while others decide mental attributes, like insight, creative ability, or disposition. A portion of the qualities are predominant; they produce the characteristic in each age. Others are passive and produce characteristics that skirt a few generations.Hair tone, for instance, is created by a prevailing quality, while jutting ears delivered by a latent quality.

The sex cell from the mother-the "ovum-is prepared by the sex cell from the dad the "spermatozoon." Before treatment can happen, both the ovum and the spermatozoon should age or develop. As a sex cell matures, it goes through a division interaction during which the 23 sets of chromosomes split. At the point when a developed cell is framed from this parting system, it contains just 23 single chromosomes in which there are 40,000 to 60,000 qualities. Assuming treatment happens, the new cell accordingly contains 46 chromosomes, half from the mother and half from the dad.

During the aging system, it is absolutely impossible to control which chromosomes with their qualities will go into each part. There are countless conceivable outcomes of blends of various physical and mental characteristics that might be given to the new child from the chromosomes he acquires. Each child's legacy is, consequently, mostly a question of possibility.

It has been said that the snapshot of origination when the female cell is prepared by the male cell - is perhaps of the main second in the whole existence of a person. The explanation being that his entire inheritance is still up in the air at that point. Never after that might he at any point get new qualities or dispose of a portion of the qualities obtained right now of origination.

Boy Or Girl

From the very start of history individuals have estimated and explored different avenues regarding the chance of controlling the sec of a child. There have likewise been various fantasies and stories associated with the control of the youngster's sec. For instance, it has been trusted that assuming origination happens soon after feminine cycle, a female kid will be conceived; assuming that a mother eats a lot of sugar during pregnancy, she will have a young lady; assuming that she eats meat in huge amounts, she will have a kid. Others have accepted that the long stretch of the year in which origination happens decides the sex of the youngster,

Researchers have invalidated this large number of speculations and practices for controlling sex. We currently realize what decides the sex of a kid, yet up to right now there is no known method for controlling sex. Sex is completely a question of possibility, with the possibilities somewhat more good for the male than tthe female sex. Measurements show that there are roughly 105 to

106 male infants brought into the world for each 100 females. Nobody knows exactly why this is so. What decides the sex of the kid is the kind of sex chromosome in the spermatozoon that prepares the ovum. Of the 23 sets of chromosomes in the spermatozoon, 22 sets are: coordinated and the twenty-third pair, comprised of two sex chromosomes, X and Y, are unique. At the point when the spermatozoon parts during the developing system, the X goes into one section and the Y into the other part. This implies that one-half of all developed spermatozoa convey the X chromosome, half convey the Y chromosome. All full grown ova convey the X chromosome.

In any treated ovum, there is dependably a X chromosome from the ovum and either a X or aY chromosome from the spermatozoon. In the event that the blend is XX, the kid will be female. If, then again, the mix is XY, the youngster will be male.

Multiple Births

Ordinarily, human moms produce each child in turn, yet once in each 87 births-as per measurements - twins are conceived. There are two unmistakably various sorts of twins, indistinguishable twins and non indistinguishable or brotherly twins. Indistinguishable twins come from a solitary ovum that parts into two sections not long after preparation, while non indistinguishable twins come from two ova delivered during a similar period and treated by two different spermatozoa.

Since indistinguishable twins come from one treated ovum, such youngsters have similar chromosomes and qualities. Subsequently, we find it genuine that in appearance indistinguishable twins are "as the same as just like twins."

Since only one spermatozoon treats one ovum to deliver two youngsters, indistinguishable twins are dependably of a similar sex, and their psychological and volatile cosmetics is essentially as comparable as their actual appearance.

On the other hand, non indistinguishable twins can be of the equivalent or of other genders. Since the chromosomes are not similar in the two ova or in the two spermatozoa, non indistinguishable twins are bound to be unexpected in physical and mental cosmetics in comparison to be indistinguishable. Trios, quadruplets, and other various births are undeniably more uncommon than twins. However, similar to twins, they might be either indistinguishable or they might be non indistinguishable. Typically in the non indistinguishable trios and quadruplets, they have come from two prepared ova, either of which have parted during the beginning phases of advancement. Thus, two of the trios might be indistinguishable and one non indistinguishable or, on account of quadruplets, a few might be indistinguishable and the others non indistinguishable.

Conduct Of The Infant

Since his muscles are delicate and his sensory system immature, the infant has zero influence over his developments. He can't turn his body, sit up, go after an item, or even direct his eyes. At the point when he takes a gander at you, one eye might turn in one course and the other eye in the other bearing. This, obviously, gives the child a strange articulation in any case, of more serious result, it implies that he can't see plainly or unmistakably. He is totally vulnerable and, when gotten, gives the feeling that he might go to pieces.

The lacking condition of the sensory system of the infant keeps him from controlling developments, however it makes him move all over when he moves one piece of his body. This is known as "mass movement" and is very energy-consuming. Indeed, even the straightforward demonstration of sucking, for instance, is joined by waving the arms, kicking the legs, wandering aimlessly the head and the body.

Most guardians to-be realize that infants are vulnerable and they are ready to attend to their children in every way under the sun. What many don't have any idea, nonetheless, is that this powerlessness is an extremely impermanent condition. Inside half a month after birth, powerlessness will start to diminish as the child's sensory system creates, as his muscles fortify, and as his bones solidify.

If guardians, particularly moms, start considering their children powerless in light of the fact that they were defenseless when they were conceived, they might be so prone to get things done for their children that they are well-suited to deny the children of the amazing chance to figure out how to get things done for themselves when their bodies and psyches are prepared for this.

A child starts to cry when he is conceived in some cases during the real course of birth. It is through the birth cry that the child's lungs are swelled with air, hence empowering him to relax interestingly. Each child has his own trademark cry. It could be unforgiving and puncturing or low and groaning. Notwithstanding, he can't tweak his cries with the outcome that it is challenging for individuals to realize what is wrong with him. His cries in all actuality do shift in force low in pitch when he is worn out and high when he is refreshed.

Good natured guidance about permitting a child to cry it out may on occasion be okay for a more seasoned child, yet it very well may be perilous guidance for a vulnerable infant. Crying is the main way a child needs to tell us that something is the matter with him. Hence, it is significant to overlook this peril signal. Overlooking an infant's cries is serious for another explanation. At the point when he cries, he in a real sense cries everywhere. Whenever allowed to deal with it, he will go through energy which is required for development and this will dial back the development interaction.

Notwithstanding his cries, the baby can deliver low, moaning sounds, for example, "eh" or "ah." These sounds are at times alluded to as "cooing." According to the drawn out perspective, these sounds are vital on the grounds that they are the establishment from which discourse ultimately creates.

The Child In The Family

Regardless of how little or how huge the family, life should change somehow with the appearance of another child. Making changes is rarely simple, however assuming the progressions are expected and made steadily, they are less problematic.

The material arrangements, generally, will take a somewhat brief period, yet the psychological changes and the progressions in conduct might meet more noteworthy obstruction. Consequently they ought to be made all the more leisurely. Each individual from the family ought to become accustomed to the possibility that there will be new liabilities that should be shared by all.

Many individuals accept that the primary conceived child achieves changes in the family. Valid, the layette that served the principal child is generally satisfactory to address the issues of the second or even the third with a couple of substitutions and a little remodel. Nonetheless, mental changes and changes in the way of behaving of the entire family should be made for each new child.

Assuming the change period is started sufficiently early, the entire family will be prepared to invite the appearance of the child. Not all issues, obviously, can be predicted or ready for, yet In the event that the significant changes issues are expected and effectively met before the child's introduction to the

world, the less significant ones can be addressed all
the more effectively as they emerge.

Chapter 3

Physical Development Of The Child

Could you perceive a child you had considered first to be a seven days old baby and next on his most memorable birthday?
On the off chance that you have watched the improvement of a child, you know how different he becomes, from one week to another and month to month.

Advancement and development during the primary year are outrageous. At no other time in life will it be as fast. In a year, the defenseless infant significantly increases his introduction to the world weight, takes care of himself, maybe even strolls. He holds a spoon. He is figuring out how to take care of himself. His facial highlights change surprisingly. Mental development is staying up with the actual turn of events. The year-old has thoughts on what he needs and is figuring out how to spread the word. He might utilize a couple of words and grasp some more.

Since a child develops and develops so much during his most memorable year, this part covers it.

Relation Of Physical Development To Mental Development

Physical and mental development are interrelated. Slow actual development is by and large joined by sluggish mental turn of events. With fast actual development, then again, there is generally a bright mental turn of events. Additionally, chronic frailty, particularly during times of quick development, stunts actual development, however it is probably going to influence mental development and later character advancement antagonistically. A wiped out child is touchy, peevish, and requesting consideration. On the off chance that chronic weakness perseveres for any time span, this conduct is probably going to form into a propensity.

A decent state of being with just at least disease during diaper days, then again, empowers the child to develop typically and to have a superior opportunity for a socially OK character. In the event that, furthermore, the home climate is great, as he becomes older, the sound child has a decent possibility of growing up to be a balanced grown-up.

Height And Weight

These two terms generally appear to go together; The first year of life is set apart by remarkable expansions in both level and weight. During the child's most memorable year, he encounters a 50% increment in level so that at one year he has a typical level of 28 to thirty inches.

After the main year, the child's development in level dials back to a typical addition of three to five inches yearly. This implies that most infants measure between milk-the principal component of the child's eating regimen. Afterward, as the eating routine contains components notwithstanding milk, weight increments come more from bone and muscle tissue than from fat tissue.

Many guardians, even today, accept that the fatter the child, the better he is. There is no logical proof to validate this conviction and much proof to show that plump children have however many illnesses as more slender infants. Moreover, there is adequate proof that fat children will quite often be fairly hindered in their engine foster ment. This is on the grounds that excess weight increases the awkwardness that is normal for all infants, even the individuals who are slender.

Body Proportions

Upon entering the world, the child is cumbersome in light of the fact that his head is relatively excessively enormous until the end of his body. This condition is one of the elements answerable for the defenselessness of the child during the principal year of life. The pieces of the body that are least evolved upon entering the world, the legs, trunk, feet, and hands-become the most, while the parts that are generally evolved - the head and arms-become relatively less. Since various pieces of the body develop at contrast ent rates, the child's appearance is continually evolving.

The whole top of the child is excessively large until the end of his body. The part that is particularly messed up is the upper part, or the mind area. This seems, by all accounts, to be significantly greater than it is, halfway in light of the fact that the facial elements are tiny and lacking and part of the way in light of the fact that the neck is essentially nonexistent. Before childhood is finished, the child grows a neck, and his small, lacking mouth and jaw become bigger as child teeth seem to give shape to his mouth and chin.The restricted bears and jutting mid-region of the little child likewise change in time. The shoulders become more extensive and the stomach district becomes complimentary. Nonetheless, subsequent to taking care of, the child's stomach will just extraordinarily and afterward Blatten out as it purges.

The little, spindly, abnormal legs and slim arms of the baby develop longer, straighter, and chubbier during the initial two years of life. In any case, over the course of growing up, arms and legs appear to be relatively excessively short until the end of the body similarly as in childhood. Upon entering the world, the hands and feet are little to such an extent that they appear to have a place with dolls instead of human~~of to human~~ children. During the primary year of life, the fingers and toes stretch and finish up with the goal that they lose their unique claw-like appearance. The centers of the hands expand, and the feet get greater both long and in width.

Young men at all ages, from birth until adulthood, have marginally bigger heads than young ladies. Previously, when it was accepted that size of head decided how much knowledge one had, the bigger heads of young men were referred to as verification of unrivaled masculine insight. Today, it is realized that insight isn't subject to the size of the head or the size of the cerebrum.

Significance Of Body Proportions

The impacts of the imbalances of the child's body are extremely broad. Unbalancedness makes it challenging for the child to control his body. The outcome is that he brings down effectively when he sits, stands, strolls, or runs. What seems, by all accounts, to be ungainliness isn't discernible to poor solid control alone yet additionally to the way that an excess of weight is in the upper piece of the body. Little hands, similar to little feet, add to ungainliness. A child's hands are neither enormous enough nor sufficiently able to clutch weighty items. Add to this the way that he has definitely less command over his muscles than a grown-up has, and you will promptly comprehend the reason why he drops and breaks things so regularly. Likewise, it requires more exertion on the child's part to get things done with his little, somewhat frail hands than it does some other time when his hands are bigger and more grounded. This is one reason why he surrenders so rapidly when he attempts to take care of himself or when he is playing with a toy, for he tires without any problem.

The Baby's Bones

Upon entering the world the baby's bones are more similar to ligament or cartilage than like bones. Continuously, all through diaper days, his bones solidify, giving the child's eating regimen a satisfactory stockpile of mineral salts. This solidifying, or "solidification," of the bones starts soon after birth and finishes not long before pubescence.

The delicate surface of a child's bones is extremely clear in the weaknesses, or "fontanels," on the child's skull. The biggest and least demanding fontanel to notice is on the highest point of the head. These weaknesses during the bones of the head consider the quick development of the cerebrum in the early long periods of life when the requirement for security of the mind tissue isn't ideal as it is later on as the kid turns out to be more dynamic. By the age of eighteen months, the child's fontanels are shut, and by two years practically every one of them are all around solidified. There are two huge realities that ought to be borne as a top priority about the bones of infants. In the first place, breaks in bones repair quickly. Second, delicate bones can be distorted without much of a stretch. A child who is allowed to lie on his back for a really long period might foster a level head rather than a head that is marginally adjusted toward the back. Unfortunate stance while sitting or standing might cause a slight arch of the spine that becomes set over time.

Notice the weird positions a child can get into and you will acknowledge how delicate his bones truly are. He can in a real sense twist in two or roll himself into a ball. See the image above.

The Baby's Teeth

The teeth are a piece of the bone development of the body and, similar to bones, they are delicate from the start. The early teeth, by and large called the child teeth or the milk teeth, are twenty in number.

They are little in size, delicate in surface, and have little, shallow roots; in this way, they often rot before they are supplanted by long-lasting teeth.

Teeth begin to shape during the third or fourth month of pregnancy, however they don't begin to emit until the child is five or a half years old. When they do begin, they eject ceaselessly at the pace of roughly one every month until the child is two or over two years of age. The outline and the chart at the highest point of this page show the inexact ages at which child teeth emit and the place of these teeth.

The age at which children cut their teeth has been viewed as undeniably less significant than the succession of ejection. At the point when there is anomaly in this grouping as on account of upper teeth emitting before lower - it is probably going to toss the jaw out of position. This may for all time influence the state of the lower part of the face and prompt the super durable teeth to be off the mark.

While it is famously trusted that "mal. impediment" or unfortunate arrangement of teeth, comes from thumb-sucking, dental specialists of today are starting to scrutinize this. Valid, thumb sucking that is persevering can make the front teeth jut and, hence, guardians are asked to deter the thumb-sucking propensity. Numerous dental specialists accept that jutting teeth and unfortunate arrangement of the upper and lower jaws come from anomaly in the succession of emission of the teeth, yet they are uncertain of what

causes the inconsistency of succession. In some cases getting teeth is joined by stomach related disturbs, loss of hunger, colds, or ear infections. Indeed, even with practically no of these unsettling influences, the child won't feel like standard yet will be drowsy or worrisome. When the gum has been penetrated and the tooth should be visible, be that as it may, he starts to be typical and energetic.

The significant thing to recall about getting teeth is the impact it has on a child's demeanor. It isn't by any stretch surprising for a child who has been basically as "great as gold" during the primary year of his life to transform into an unstable, crabby, and difficult to oversee baby. This is a propensity that he has persisted from long stretches of torment and uneasiness he encountered while he was getting teeth.

Illness In Babyhood

For the initial four to a half year of life, the child has a time of relative resistance to sickness. From that point on, he is probably going to have an undeniably enormous number of respiratory and gastrointestinal diseases. Infants have more respiratory aggravations throughout the cold weather months and more gastrointestinal ailments when it is sweltering. Infants from families where guardians can manage the cost of additional time, consideration, and clinical consideration for them. have less diseases than infants who don't enjoy such benefits.

Notwithstanding present day clinical strategies, inoculation, and new medications, mortality during the primary year of life is still excessively high. One of the significant purposes behind this is that many guardians don't understand how rapidly a minor sickness in a child can become serious. a grown-up moves past minor illnesses rapidly, many guardians expect that a child will likewise.

Be that as it may, this isn't accurate 100% of the time. In childhood a minor disease might form quickly into a difficult sickness with numerous confusions except if brief therapy is given. A slight temperature toward the beginning of the day. for instance, may rush to disturbing levels during the evening.

It is to be expected for a child to contract one of the kids' illnesses, like measles, mumps, chicken pox, or German measles, in the event that a sibling or sister has one of these illnesses. Youngsters' illnesses are not so serious for more established kids, particularly today when the new strategies for inoculation and the new medications are so generally utilized. Nonetheless, they are intense for a child, part of the way since few infants have been vaccinated against them and mostly on the grounds that the fever that goes with these illnesses is probably going to rise alarmingly in a child.

Hence, at whatever point there is a plague of one of the kids' sicknesses in the area or school, it is shrewd to get a child far from close contact with his more seasoned family until the risk of getting the illness has passed. The specialist ought to be counseled on the double to see how can be forestalled the child's getting the infection or to limit its seriousness assuming he has proactively contracted it.

It is some of the time vital, on account of a difficult disease, for the child to be hospitalized. This is typically a genuinely upsetting encounter for the child as well with respect to his folks. Numerous emergency clinics today give spots to moms of children to remain in the medical clinic with their infants. In the event that this is unimaginable, the mother or father ought to invest however much energy as could reasonably be expected there to take out the close to home strain which concerns the child's recuperation.

At each age, yet particularly in childhood, the familiar saying, "addressing the issue beforehand is better than addressing any aftermath later," ought to be applied. Since minor aggravations can form into serious ones so rapidly, the specialist ought to be called at whatever point the child is hot, won't eat, is

irritable, or cries more than expected. In the event
that he can't analyze the difficulty via phone, a visit
is a wise speculation since it might address the
difficulty before it becomes major.

One more significant part of anticipation is to take
the child for occasional tests in the specialist's
office, regardless of whether he is by all accounts
entirely well. Normally exams are more regular
during the first than during the second year of the
child's life.

What To Do About Crying

The call of an exceptionally youthful child ought to
be regarded; he has not yet figured out how to cry
only for consideration. It could be a wet diaper, a
late bubble, a draft or overheated state of his room,
or unappeased hunger that is making him
self-conscious. Friendship is as much a need

food and rest. In the event that he wakes around
midnight, a consoling pat relieving voice is some of
the time all he wants. A few children need more

close consideration than others. On the off chance that the child requires it, the mother might remain with him somewhat longer than expected when she takes care of him. Singing, tapping him, at times shaking him, or working about his room a short time will assist with loosening up him to the place of sluggishness.

As he becomes older, the sort of cry might demonstrate the idea of his message"- depression, torment, or tired objecting. A mother figures out how to perceive the distinction between sob for help and gentle dissent c fastidiousness.

Unfortunate propensities are in some cases encouraged by the negligent mother who tends~~tend~~ to make the child's requirements since it gives her pleasure. Getting him when he cries or spoiling every one of his impulses imparts a disposition that hampers his whole friendly change. Crying turns into his standard method for communicating this mentality.

Chapter 4

Emotional And Social Development

Have you at any point asked why a circumstance produces different profound reactions in individual kids? What compels peter burst
 into rage assuming mother's esteemed doll is taken from him, while Paul only grins and surrenders it eagerly? For what reason does Susy shout and kick the kitchen cupboard on the off chance that mother says, "No, a treat will kill your desire to eat for supper. We'll eat in only a couple of moments," yet this equivalent rebuke brings a suitable "OK" from James as he returns to his play for those couple of moments.

Why these various responses? For what reason does one kid appear to be essentially amiable, another crotchety, one enthusiastic, another tranquil; one lively, one bleak? Will they remain so? Could we at any point impact positive mentalities and reactions? Assuming this is the case, how?

Introduction

In the previous area you found out about actual improvement during the principal year of life. In the part close to this you will find out about the scholarly turn of events. Both of these periods of youngster development can more promptly be noticed and checked than can profound and social turn of events. Truly, we have various guideposts; "see" a kid develop. Scholarly development can be seen in the youngster's extending abilities to think, reason and comprehend; once more, we can "see" proof of mental development.

Following profound advancement in children is really difficult. Frequently, regardless of whether noticed, it is to a great extent misjudged. The age among birth and three years is especially obligated to misconception and bungle. Why?Generally on the grounds that we will more often than not relegate our own sentiments or feelings to the youngster. Many guardians give the kid's singular necessities practically zero thought. Kids just "become " harmonious, or peaceful, or bad tempered.

Absence of seeing frequent results since we neglect to perceive a kid's age level and development. We attempt to utilize grown-up guidelines. Conduct of Little kids might be impeccably n mal for their own age to adults who expect youngsters go about as "little grown-ups" instead of a the little experimenters that they are

The nine-month-old child who is discriminately biting on broken entryway stops, and papers is essentially answering a need to investigate and learn. To him everything is shiny, new and invigorating; everything should be dealt with, tasted, or banged. He should learn along these lines; and we should safeguard him-as opposed to our entryway stops or papers while he learns.
A few grown-ups are of the assessment that a youngster's social development is invigorated primarily by his from home openness contacts, to a great extent initiating with school. This is

profoundly wrong. Assuming we are to really comprehend and direct a kid, we return to the day of his introduction to the world and, surprisingly, further back. The foundation of his home and the homes of every one of his folks is important here. A child is brought into the world with specific capacities with regards to development of his heredity. Heredity decides as far as possible inside which a youngster can create. Envi Instigate shapes and impacts the improvement which really happens. These powers cooperate; not one or the other can be totally free of the other. Heredity tracks down articulation through climate: climate impacts the improvement of acquired attributes

The initial two years of life are vital in friendly and close to home turn of events. Character designs are shown once in a while "set" by age a few; others are as yet changing at six or as youths. Some are rarely totally shaped.

There are arrangements close to home advancement as in physical and engine improvement. While these groupings are essential for all youngsters, a child's singular turn of events and it be completely his own to time will. One child will adapt to his specific responsive qualities, stresses, and close to home

strains in a totally different manner than another.
Each brings to a circumstance his own distinction.
For instance, all infants answer an unexpected
shaking of the surface on which they are lying.
Nonetheless, after the main yanking development,
one child will shout, an other will wriggle a bit, and
another will rapidly recapture his com

No two infants grow precisely indistinguishable.
You will study profound contrasts as you read. The
significant thing to remember is that-as in actual
improvement the general example for all children is
something similar, yet inside this example, each
grows genuinely in his own specific manner.

What Is Personality?

Personality is the aggregate of explicit attributes
(like timidity or brightness) that are perceptibly
steady in a singular's way of behaving. To be steady,
the way of behaving character is available
throughout some undefined time frame and in
changed exercises. A forceful quality, for instance,
might be credited to the child who gets himself after

a tumble and attempts once more, who commotions boisterously for his food when not quickly impending, and who over and over attempts to get under the couch to recover his ball, in spite of the chances against him.

Character qualities are a large number. The levels of every attribute modest, incidentally bashful, exceptionally timid, horrendously timid grant endless varieties. Shy individuals might be despondent, however not really so; one can be bashful, yet happy and stable-another forceful, yet satisfied and stable. Hostility may as promptly be joined by insecurity. In spite of the fact that there is no set example in blends of qualities, certain qualities truly do show up together habitually enough to give backing to the reason that there is an overall solidarity to specific propensities. Clinician Gordon Allport makes a valid statement of this in Character. We tend to "type" individuals by broad examples.

Character attributes are not steady all of the time. A youngster need not stay inside the example of his initial turn of events. A tentative, unfortunate young person might be assisted with turning out to be more certain and secure. Then again, qualities encouraged by serious, persistent encounters right off the bat in life might establish such areas of strength that must be modified with trouble, at times never. Relentless patterns in character results from genetic, early encounters and constantly repeating conditions. A youngster's later private and adjustive conduct will be the final product.

Factors Influencing Emotional And Social Development

Mothering

Mothering is the single, most powerful impact in close to home turn of events. The mindful individual need not be the child's mom; it could be a temporary mother, great. mother, a more established sister, or even a dad. More significant is that the mother-individual is tender and reliable. "Mothering" should be warm, authentic, and ceaseless.

The main language a baby comprehends during the primary long stretches of life is the material contact of the mother or individual really focusing on him. Actual consideration influences him mentally.

There is implicit correspondence between even an extremely youthful child and his mom. His close to home state is an unobtrusive reflection and continuation of her own. On the off chance that she is quiet, loose, and blissful, the child will feel more satisfied and secure. Indeed, even an apparently irrelevant thought, for example, how a child is held conveys explicit impressions to him. A certain mother will snuggle her child, handle him solidly, and converse with him soothingly.

Most new moms are bungling and apprehensive from the outset, yet an over-restless mother, concerned in case the thing she is doing may not be correct, spreads her nervousness and uncertainty. She isn't as liable to talk soothingly and merrily during his shower or diapering, His crying unduly concerns her Throughout the long term, her demeanor in-wrinkles his crabbiness; his peevishness builds her anxiety. Consequently, the unending cycle summons reactions that might become constant. For this rea-child, clinicians are of the assessment that a portion of the distinctions in characters of the first and second chil-dren in a family are expected to some degree to the expanded certainty with which a mother really focuses on her subsequent youngster Understanding what to do gives security which is given to the child.

This doesn't imply that a child needs an ideal mother for an ideal turn of events. That would be excessive. Most new moms go through a learning period; all have dissatisfactions, highs and lows, steadiness and shakiness. Indeed, even the best, best intentioned guardians have slips, yet except if rehashed often they cause no extraordinary damage. Human instinct is fundamentally adaptable. It is the guardians' pretty much long-lasting, predictable demeanor that is imparted to the child. The circumstances encouraging trust are those normally existing in any home where guardians care for each other and their kids, where they put forth an earnest attempt to cherish and safeguard their youngsters in their own specific manner.

Absence Of Mothering

Similarly as the presence of affection and mothering helps a youngster "blossom" inwardly, its extreme absence stunts profound development. Indeed, even a minuscule child feels dejected. At the point when let be the majority of his waking hours however actual necessities are met-a newborn child neglects to become responsive. Proceeding with absence of excitement brings about lack of care. This is particularly evident in kids restricted to ineffectively staffed establishments. Generic, in continuous consideration brings about removed and lethargic perspectives. These youngsters have no specific individual whom they can call their own. They have nobody to adore; therefore. they have not fostered the limit with respect to ordinary connections.

The scientists Dennis and Dennis revealed, because of investigations of kids in Lebanon shelters, that they accepted the sort of grown-up focusing on the baby was a higher priority than the actual climate, whether it be home or establishment.

Over-mothering

While a baby needs practically complete insurance and care for the initial eight or nine months of his life, he arrives at a phase where it is possible to over-safeguard or over-mother him. Close to ten months or a year, when he starts to "do" for himself in eating, strolling, and playing, mother ought to give up a piece of his requirement for her. She ought to perceive and empower his rising freedom, assisting him with happening to his next period of advancement.

Emotional Environment
Of His Home

Friendship and concordance between guardians goes about as the establishment on which an effective family is constructed. Add to this affection and comprehension of every youngster as an individual, and have ideal circumstances for social close to home turn of events. From birth, a baby ought to be viewed as an individual from the family bunch, not the focal point of consideration, but rather concurred a situation in a legitimate viewpoint to other relatives.

Human relations in the home significantly impact profound turn of events. As expressed already, mother's is of introductory significance for she is nearest to the child during his most memorable weeks, really focusing on his requirements. Inside a couple of months, different individuals from his family progressively took part in his exercises. They resemble a mirror where a child sees himself. He starts to gain sentiments about himself from the manner in which others answer him. Their mentalities apply as strongly an effect on development of his character as genuine encounters. For example, his impressions of his family and their absolute relations toward him will influence his close to home development much more than whether and for how long he is breastfed, whether his toys are

of the best or unremarkable quality, or whether his play region is a playpen or a sweeping on the floor. Mentally, families don't have similar guardians. Blends of qualities are unique. Every youngster has a one of a kind hereditary example and will answer in various ways to what has all the earmarks of being a similar climate. Each will be affected by the differing ways family members and companions feel about him, address him, and treat him. Perhaps he is a more seasoned sibling or a more youthful sibling; not the equivalent, right? Also, guardians and youngsters change as they become older. Mentalities change, as well. Each has various encounters. These encounters are associated with the singular heredity example of It makes sense of the large number of characters inside a similar family, inside evidently a similar climate.

Emotions Of The Child

It is hard to tell whether the crying of a fourteen day old child is provoked by dread, outrage, craving, or agony. The declarations of feeling appear to be all indistinguishable; responses are outrageous. Upon entering the world, as per K. M. B. Spans in Kid Advancement, "fervor is the main close to home express." The infant is either calm or restless, agreeable or awkward.

These similarly purposeless and undiscriminating reactions of extravagance steadily accept structures that can be perceived. Development and experience assist a child with putting himself out there better. Constantly month, the child produces various cries to communicate various things: appetite, agony, or inconvenience.

Explicit reactions create as the child interfaces his sentiments with outside conditions and interior sensations or reflexes. He perceives developments, lights, and sounds. He likewise has "reports' ' from his own body. Child can not converse and educate us how he feels concerning things in any case, throughout the long term, we can see extremely unequivocal changes in his way of behaving, showing that his sentiments, as well, have acquired precision and clearness of framework.

At 90 days, the child shows de light, misery, and energy. After a half year, trouble has been refined and separated into unmistakable trepidation, repugnance, or outrage. By a year, enchant is explained further into joy and warmth. Certain feelings are unmistakable in most year old enfants. We will go through some of them.

Amusement

The tapping, stroking, and nestling of a grown-up child's approach to showing joy and joy come to have significance to the baby. Mother's delicate touch stimulates sentiments in which lie the fundamentals of delight and, later, warmth and joy. Before long, something like two months, he grins at mother. He communicates internal joy, a sensation of sharpness and prosperity, yet doesn't connect joy with outside things. He kicks, beats his arms, blows air pockets and grins brilliantly in light of the fact that he feels better.

At four months he moves energized when he sees food coming; he sprinkles and crows with joy in his shower: he answers father's voice in the event that he hopes to be held and made over at a specific time; he considen splendid, moving items with consumed interest. He snickers resoundingly because of a cooing voice, dreary, chirruping sounds, or brilliant looks. At ten months, the child's entire body conveys joy. He bangs toys enthusiastically on his high seat or the floor feet kick happily; eyes dance. shenanigans are joined by kick blocks of pleasure. Child might go after the wellspring of his enjoyment, and in the event that it's mom's face, she might track down her hair, nose, or cheek got a handle on in a little clench hand, for child needs to feel the pleasurable item

Distress

DistressDustress is incited by hunger, torment, failure,or depression. The extremely youthful child responds unpredictably and with uniform power whether it be for a postponed taking care of or excruciating colic. The brutality of the response doesn't demonstrate the idea of his irritation; it is overstated and plentiful. Crying, kicking and pushing of arms and legs, on the other hand opening and gripping toes and fingers, demonstrate irritation in a truly earth-shattering way. He develops red and sifts about.

At four months, trouble is as yet abundant yet more promptly checked. Child might cry robustly however stop suddenly at being gotten or calmed. Term of crying starts to be in relation to the reason. Responses start to separate as indicated by the justification for his misery. Misery will be refined into unmistakable apprehension, outrage, or revulsion by a half year.

Fear

For the initial half year of the child's life, he can't see danger; in this manner he responds just with fervor or misery.

Fear creates when we have no palatable approach to meeting a danger. It vanishes when we understand what to do and how to adapt to it. Thus, a child of a few months shows no reaction or feeling of dread toward a weird face. By a half year, his developing limits see the newness of another face whose goals are obscure and he responds with timidity or withdrawal, a normal response to fear.

Outrage

Early appearance of outrage, recognizable at a half year, results from disappointment of wants or impedance of objectives. Outrage is regularly shown during washing or dressing. To the child, being held limited is disturbing. Early articulations are diffuse, unstable, and undirected, an appalling presentation of temper. Inside a couple of months, he starts to perceive his cutoff points and acknowledges a few limitations to satisfy his longings. He has some origin of power. His resilience increases, empowering him to adapt to some defer in his need. fulfilled, certain that this is over in a short while. Around multi month outrage is more controlled, coordinated against the hindrance or wrongdoer. Toward the finish of the principal year, outrage incites an assault reaction, striking, slapping, gnawing, or kicking the article or individual starting it.

Fondness

Early cooing, grinning, and sputtering are not signs
of love, but rather the heralds of this inclination.
Child is building po tive profound inclinations
toward individuals who give security and feline to
his necessities, however he stays on the less than
desirable finish of warmth for the greater part of

the principal year. He may properly answer
solicitations to kiss or embrace mother or another
relative, yet he is just completing an idea.

Slowly, his sentiments progres from simple need and
inner self fulfillment to appreciation, steadfastness,
and-later defense. At one year, he was fit for starting
love. At the point when he offers it, he frequently
separates, showing inclination for one individual
over another.

Embracing, cuddling into a sho der, stroking,
needing to be he by his "number one," or moving in
a lap are normal exhibits might go to track down
mother, beat on leg for consideration, be guaranteed

by b reaction, and afterward be content to back to his play after this consolation. He might communicate friendship when Daddy gets back home by embracing his dad's leg until he is conveyed up.

Chapter 5

Intellectual Development

We aren't aware as much about a baby's psychological advancement as we are at the same time, initiating with the main arbitrary way of behaving upon entering the world, we notice scholarly development. In the somewhat brief time of outset, much obvious headway is made.

Mental development can't start to be dependably tried until about two years old. And, after it's all said and done, unwavering quality is low. Nobody can precisely anticipate future scholarly execution based on tests at age two and three. Up to that point, it is demonstrated primarily in substantial controls and engine achievements.

The Brain And Its Capabilities

The focal sensory system incorporates the mind and the spinal string. vertebrae or "spine," capabilities as a pathway for motivations between the body and the mind. For instance, assuming you slam your toe, fringe or "station" nerves send this message to the line and on to the mind. Inside a brief instant, your mind gets, interprets, and coordinates activity, maybe a vocal "Oof!"

Explicit regions of the mind have explicit capabilities. The frontal cortex, or the front piece of the mind, is partitioned into a few segments, one of which handles approaching driving forces: one more registers and concludes what move to initiate on these motivations: an-other sends the choices to the muscles and organs. The cerebellum enormous side region of the mind arranges smooth muscle development and keeps up with body harmony, stance, and muscle tone. The cortex, or external layer of the cerebrum, is significant for learning and the acquisition of additional mind boggling capacities. "Cortex" in a real sense signifies "bark": that is, the external covering of a tree. Your memorable ability and previous involvement with the radiance of new circumstances is a component of the cortex.

The cortex is by and large viewed as latent upon entering the world and for a month or so from there on. It creates at a similar age more leisurely than different segments of the mind. Nonetheless, its improvement is vital before a baby can figure out how to sit, creep, or execute other coordinated abilities that require incorporated developments. The cortex is totally developed by two years. Fundamental engine capacities are created during this period: they structure a heap for later exercises and solutions of muscles.

How A Child Learns

Learning is a double course of mental and actual development. Such development or development as examined before - follows a characteristic succession or steps. While the grouping is genuinely consistent for all children, the timing (precise age when a stage happens) and the energy or capacity applied to any one stage are totally personal. One kid will outperform one more in understanding and talking, similarly as a youngster might figure out how to walk or deal with his food better at a similar age.

 Development and development remain inseparable. Assuming a baby only developed size, he would not be able to sit, wall or figure out how to talk. Size ought to be just a single standard for passing judgment on capacities however three-month-old Peter weighs over half year old Paul, who can sit alone, Billy can't be anticipated to do likewise. His development has not achieved the fundamental transformative phase: at 90 days his head is excessively huge and weighty and his body; his neck muscles are not sufficiently able to help it for sitting. He has not obtained adequate adjusting ability for adjusting, and his back muscles are as yet frail.

Many guardians are unduly concerned when their kid is contrasted and a neighbor's youngster who does things early . Late engine achievements don't guarantee sub-par mental capacity.

Chapter 6

Children Sickness

In any event, for new born children, sickness in the preschool years is more normal than it will be as the kid becomes older and, surprisingly, more normal, however undeniably less serious, than it is in diaper days. The justification for the more successive ailment in youth than in diaper days is that the child can be preferably directed in his exercises over the small kid can, particularly when he is playing outside with different youngsters. In the event that, for instance, the little child is strolling in the city with his mom, she can direct him away from puddles of water. At the point when, then again, the small kid is playing with his companions, in the event that one proposes it would be enjoyable to get around the puddles, he might land in a puddle, get wet feet, and not change his shoes or socks until he gets back an hour or all the more later. The following morning he has a sneeze or an irritated throat.

Diseases in youth need not be serious in the event that the kid is in a decent state of being and in the event that immediate consideration is offered to any hint of sickness by his folks. Most guardians, having found how rapidly a minor all men transformed into a high fever or other upsetting side effects when the kid was a child, will generally be mindful at times over careful.

The previous diagram shows the normal ailments of youth in the request for recurrence of events. Note how normal the basic colds, respiratory illnesses, and stomach related disturbances are as contrasted and the infectious illnesses. In a family where there could be no more seasoned kids, the small kid is less inclined to get a dis-ease like measles or chickenpox than he is at the point at which he goes to class.

While few small kids get away from disease, some appear to have too much. These youngsters are frequently alluded to as ailment inclined. There are many purposes behind disease inclination in youth. Some chil-dren are not generally so sound as others either due to unfortunate heredity conditions or poor actual consideration from the hour of birth. More small kids, it has been found. who have a progression of diseases come from homes where healthful necessities are not m and where parental consideration is less fortunate than valid for those of better home environment. Young ladies are once in a while more sick than young men. This isn't on the grounds that young ladies are better and more grounded than young men in any case, rather, in light of the fact that young men do more stupid things than young ladies. They will, for instance, not wear rubbers when it showers since they don't need other boja to think they are sissies.

Numerous small kids who appear to have too many ailments are not sick; they simply envision that they are. Such kids have found, from previous encounters, that they can certainly stand out and can more readily try not to do things they truly do like to do when they are sick than when they are well. When in this way, they are confronted with accomplishing something they would rather not do, as going to nursery the everyday schedule to go, they whine that they don't feel great,

Nonexistent disease is definitely more uncommon in small kids than in more seasoned however it is sufficiently normal to be serious. Moreover, in the event that it begins in youth, it can and frequently forms into a difficult issue as the kid becomes older. A large number of the school fears of kids where they won't go where they have serious emotional mal eruptions joined by heaving to school and other actual side effects of disease, begin from nonexistent illnesses in youth.

Hospitalization Of Children

There is a developing inclination to send kids to a medical clinic either a medical clinic restricted to the consideration of youngsters or an exceptional part of an overall medical clinic at whatever point the specialist feels that extraordinary consideration is required when he is anxious about the possibility that that a minor disease might form into a more serious one.

Then, at that point, as well, with the need for the overwhelming majority of small kids to have their tonsils and adenoids eliminated due to their unhealthy version, a short stay in the clinic for argory is fundamental. Should the youngster have a mishap which brings about a wrecked bone or cuts that require lines, many specialists require the kid to stay in the medical clinic for 24 hours or more until they are certain the youngster has recuperated from the shock of the mishap or until the chance of contamination has passed. Barely any American child of today can hope to circumvent going to the medical clinic, in any event, for just a short term visit, before they arrive at the young

To most youngsters, going to the medical clinic is a startling in the event that not a frightening encounter This is expected, to a limited extent, to their anxiety toward being away from the natural environmental elements of the home and from their folks and, to some degree, to the way that they have heard, or seen on television, in comics, or in the films specialists and attendants who appear to be cutting up individuals.

Since dread can disrupt the advantages of the treatment the youngster can get in an emergency clinic, most guardians today are allowed or encouraged to invest energy with the kid in the medical clinic until he becomes acquainted with the normal therapy he will get there. Other well known approaches to meeting the trepidation issues consist of advising the youngster what's in store in the method of routine consideration while he is in the emergency clinic and of placing him in a ward or a semi-private room where he will have the friendship of different kids.

Should the youngster need extraordinary consideration which will require being in a confidential room, one parent ought to orchestrate to remain with the kid constantly until it is clear that the kid has changed alright to the weirdness of the medical clinic not to be genuinely upset on the off chance that the parent leaves for a brief time frame.

Mental Effects Of Illness

The mental impacts of ailment are frequently more noteworthy and more persevering than the actual impacts. Sickness requires an adjustment of the small kid's daily schedule. He dozes and wakes when he feels like it, whether around mid-afternoon or night. His current circumstance is limited to his room. He should rest discreetly in bed or be set up in a seat, Consequently, his play should be confined to any exercises he can continue without moving around.

As an insurance, different youngsters are not allowed to play with him, and he should depend upon himself or the grown-ups of the family for entertainment. This break in his deeply grounded routine before long becomes monotonous, and he is probably going to become unstable and peevish. As he recuperates, he is progressively irritated by the restrictions forced upon him. The youngster's mentality changes as disease powers an adjustment of his way of behaving. He requests more consideration than expected; he finds he can have his own specific manner; he frets and cries since his mom is anxious about the possibility that that worrying and crying might exacerbate him, and he finds that wickedness isn't rebuffed as it is the point at which he is well.

On the off chance that he doesn't feel good, he is paused and entertained. This amounts to one serious truth to be specific, that he is being ruined. Indeed, even after a short disease, it will require investment for a small kid to get back to business as usual. The youngster who has become ruined while hostility hopes to be the focal point of consideration when he is all around ok to get back to the play bunch in the area or in nursery the everyday schedule. This will generally make different kids won't play with him since he is so nosy. Likewise, while he is sick, his close companions might obtain new play abilities which he has not had a valuable chance to learn. They may, for instance, have figured out how to ride tricycles or bikes, how to roller skate, how to play police and burglars, or how to swim. At the point when he gets back to play with them, after his recuperation, he won't know how to play as they do. This, additional to his bossy demeanor, will generally make him an unwanted individual from the play bunch in which he previously was a cheerful and very much acknowledged member.

Common Physical Defects

Actual deformities which, in diaper days, appeared to be excessively minor to make any meaningful difference with, may turn out to be more serious and more debilitating as the kid becomes older. The youngster may, likewise, foster a few new imperfections either in the fallout of a disease or a mishap. Then again, a portion of the deformities which guardians dreaded were serious may clear up as the youngster becomes older, while others might be controlled or killed by clinical consideration before they become serious.

A youngster who appeared to have great hearing or vision as a child may, as he becomes older, experience difficulty with his eyes or ears. As his eyeballs develop, surrenders in vision not thought before may show up. Or on the other hand, great hearing in diaper days might give way to halfway deafness because of an ear contamination not treated soon to the point of trying not to have the eardrum cracked. As the child's eating regimen extends, food he previously didn't eat may end up being the wellspring of asthma, hives, c other hypersensitive responses.

At whatever stage in life, actual imperfections are serious, both from the physical and from the psycho sensible point. A youngster who has an actual imperfection that disrupts his exercises has a unique risk since it denies him of the activity required for typical development while, simultaneously, making him subject to others for help at the age when kids are particularly restless to figure out how to be free. It is likewise significant to have a deformity that obstructs his capacity to be dynamic since it denies him chances to accompany different kids and to play the difficult games they appreciate.

Assuming the youngster has an imperfection that damages his engaging quality, for example, a slight twisting of his lips because of an uncorrected harelip or a scar from a mishap, it won't irritate him except if his folks and close friends remark about it. How they respond to it will decide how he will respond to it. In the event that guardians are clearly concerned and give their very best to disguise the imperfection the kid will become unsure about it similarly as he will on the off chance that his close companions ask him what is wrong with his face or allude to his entertaining mouth. Then again, assuming they disregard it, so will he.

Chapter 7

Childhood Accidents

Most non-lethal mishaps are brought about by tumbles from level, with most passes happening because of fire.

A youngster can be harmed anyplace in or around the home, yet the most well-known place for mishaps to happen is in the residing or lounge area. The most serious mishaps happen in the kitchen and on the steps.

There are possible dangers in each home, like high temp water, family synthetics, chimneys and sharp articles. The plan of certain homes, like those with galleries and open flights of stairs, can likewise add to mishaps.

Small kids can't evaluate the dangers that these things present. Their view of the climate around them is much of the time restricted and their absence of involvement and improvement, like unfortunate coordination and equilibrium, can bring about them being harmed. Mishaps can happen whenever of the day, however they're bound to happen in the late evening and afternoon. Most youngsters have mishaps throughout the mid year, at ends of the week and during school occasions.

There are various elements that can add to a physical issue in the home, including:

- Interruption and unfortunate oversight.
- Changes to the youngster's typical daily practice or being in a rush.
- Unfortunate lodging and stuffed conditions (adolescence mishaps are firmly connected to social hardship).

- Being new to environmental factors, for example, when on vacation or while visiting companions or family members.

Chapter 8

Acquiring Skills

A skill is a progression of developments including the coordination of nerves and muscles which has been learned through rehashed practice. When an expertise is very much mastered, the body will complete the exercises in a programmed, machine-like way without conscious thoughtfulness regarding the demonstrations by the person. No youngster is brought into the world with abilities: they should be learned

Notwithstanding the time and exertion expected to master abilities, the kid should do. Skills make him free of grown-up help and they empower him to entertain himself without depending upon others to do. Considerably more significant, abilities are vital for the youngster's socialization. As friendly contacts between youngsters are essentially restricted to play, the kid who comes up short on abilities expected to play with different kids will find half an unwanted individual from the play

Undeniably the most important resource of abilities is the impact they have on the youngster's character. Each kid passes judgment on himself by contrast and different youngsters in the things he does. In the event that he can ride a tricycle better than they can, toss a ball further, or draw an image that different kids or grown-ups respect, it provides him with an identity significance and fearlessness. If, on the

Then again, he is ungainly and off-kilter in doing things his agemates do easily. How might he feel that he is everything except substandard compared to them?

Childhood The Brilliant Age To Acquire Skills

Youth has been known as the brilliant age for gaining abilities the best opportunity to figure out how to do whatever number things as could be allowed. Gaining abilities is a good time for a kid, and he partakes in the steady reiteration required for learning. He is courageous as contrasted and more seasoned youngsters and will): have a go at anything. Moreover, he has no con abilities to obstruct the new ones, and this makes it simpler for him to learn.

Just the straightforward abilities, notwithstanding, ought to be mastered during youth. They are the establishments for the better abilities. Until they are all around dominated, it will be unimaginable for the youngster to gain proficiency with the abilities expected for better muscle coordination. It is an instance of "figuring out how to stroll prior to figuring out how to run."

No youngster, for instance, can be anticipated to figure out how to compose with a pencil until he has figured out how to control his arm and hand and endures a very long time of training in jotting, drawing, and painting with the utilization of pastels, paints, and pencils.

Essentials In Acquiring Skills

There are six significant fundamentals to mastering an expertise, not one of which can be overlooked in the event that the ability is to be mastered effectively. These fundamentals are displayed underneath;

- Availability to learn.
- A powerful urge to learn.
- Potential chances to rehearse.
- A decent model to mimic.
- Practice until the ability is all around mastered.
- Direction and oversight to guarantee practice of the right kind.

As was focused on before a kid can't learn until his psyche and body have developed enough for him to learn. Nor will needing to learn be sufficient. He should have chances to rehearse the ability until he has dominated it. There is a well-known axiom that "Careful discipline brings about promising results." This is valid provided that the youngster rehearses under direction and management to safeguard that he is rehearsing in the correct manner and provided that he is emulating a decent model.

Indeed, even a decent model isn't sufficient except if he has direction in how to copy this model. A youngster figures out how to get things done by watching others and by copying what they do. He can't at first duplicate totally the developments made by someone else, and he may not actually see exactly how the move-ments are made, particularly in the event that the individual he is replicating moves excessively fast,

If, nonetheless, the individual he is attempting to duplicate moves gradually, and assuming that he is checked when he copies any development mistakenly, the kid will then, at that point, know how to continue to prepare his body to make comparable developments.

Since kids advance by impersonation, it is fundamental that the grown-up he utilizes as a model be comparable to conceivable. An unfortunate beginning, coming about because of copying an unfortunate model, may mean an inadequately mastered expertise, or it might require relearning the whole expertise. It is similarly as simple for a kid to copy a decent model as an unfortunate one, however it is difficult for him to learn in the event that he gets everything rolling in the incorrect manner.

How significant a decent model is, particularly when joined with direction and management until the model is imitated accurately, might be found in play abilities. Most small kids gain their play abilities from impersonating different youngsters and without direction subsequently, they frequently foster abilities in the incorrect way which holds them back from becoming bosses as they become older. It is an instance of the "clueless leaders leading their clueless followers"

Speech Skills

Of all skills a kid should master, the most troublesome is speech. This isn't the only one since talking includes control of the better muscles of the lips, tongue, and vocal system, yet in addition it includes figuring out how to connect implications with the words verbally expressed. The focuses of the cerebrum that control this capability the "affiliation area" mature later than the areas that control body developments. Discourse is consequently an engine mental expertise rather than simply an engine ability.

Despite the fact that the kid is maturationally unready to figure out how to talk until his most memorable birthday, he has method for correspondence
through cries and motions. His most memorable words, while deciphered by guardians to imply that he has begun to talk, are normally parrot discourse. The child copies straightforward words he has heard others use and talks them accurately yet there is no sign that he understands what they mean.

Afterward, would it be advisable for him to gain proficiency with "canine" and afterward allude to all creatures, felines, pony or lions-as canines, you can be extremely sure that he still has a lot still to find out about talking. Just when he articulates a word accurately and partners the right significance with it has begun to dominate the troublesome expertise of talking.

Understanding What Others Say

At the point when a child initially hears words, they are totally useless to him. In time, he finds out about the thing being said by watching the looks of the speaker. A grin on the essence of the speaker comes to mean endorsement, while an irate look implies dissatisfaction.

Likewise, words said frequently enough have a recognizable sound to the youngster, however he doesn't really have the foggiest idea what they mean until some affiliation is made between the words and individuals or things they address. Consequently, in conversing with a child or a small kid, it is crucial to show him word implications by naming things. For instance, "cup" turns into a significant word when the grown-up focuses on a cup and articulates "cup" at the same time.

At the point when grown-ups understand that each word they use is good for nothing to a youngster until the kid learns the significance by affiliation, they will see the value in the fact that it means quite a bit to the kid to have help in dominating this troublesome undertaking.

Aids In Understanding

- Talk gradually and particularly with the goal that the has opportunity and willpower to get a handle on the significance of the various words.
- Utilize a less difficult word.
- Whenever a recognizable word can be filled in for a new one, do as such.
- Assuming the kid shows that a word is insignificant to him, rehash it and make sense of the significance.

What Amount Does A Child Fathom?

Investigations of huge gatherings of infants and small kids provides us some insight with respect to how much perception we can expect at various ages. Translation of looks and signals starts around the age of 90 days. At half a year, the child ought to perceive his own name, and when he is eighteen months old, the importance of such basic inquiries as "Are you languid?" or "Are you hungry?" ought to be perceived. A half year after the fact, the kid ought to grasp basic orders, for example, "Come to supper" or "Toss me the ball."

From the age of two, the youngster's perception will grow quickly. At each age, nonetheless, his perception jargon will be more prominent than his utilization jargon. That is, he will know the significance of additional words than he really utilizes. How huge his understanding jargon is, thusly, will rely cautiously upon individuals who are

with him to assist him with learning word
implications.

Social Values Of Speech

An ungainly and abnormal Similarly as a kid
becomes reluctant and creates sensations of
individual insufficiency, so does the child whose
speech is mediocre compared to that of his
agemates. On the off chance that he talks so gravely
that he can't be perceived or then again assuming he
can't comprehend what others are endeavoring to tell
him, he feels cut off from individuals and desolate.
While his folks might have the option to
comprehend what he says assuming he talks
babytalk or then again in the event that he falters,
different youngsters may not. Besides, they will
prod him since he "talks like a child" or they will
giggle at his interesting discourse in the event that
he falters or stammers.

The child who becomes reluctant about his
discourse before long chooses to keep quiet

whenever the situation allows. In time, he forms into a nontalker, a quiet Sam. This is a particular social impediment. On the off chance that he can't or won't contribute his portion to what his close friends are talking about, they will overlook him. In school, the youngster who has fostered the propensity for being a nontalker will give the feeling that he knows short of what he does. Since discourse assumes such a significant part in the youngster's life, no time, exertion, or direction ought to be saved in making it comparable to conceivable, And, on the grounds that any expertise can best be mastered with cautious direction by a grown-up, instructing a to talk and to talk accurately ought to be one of the significant obligations of his folks.

Chapter 9

The Child's Responsibility

Responsibilities Regarding His Space

A large part of the joy as well as a large part of the mental worth of his very own position will come from the youngster's liability regarding it. Obviously, a small kid can't be anticipated to take on full obligation, however most little youngsters are equipped for taking on more obligation than they are offered a chance to expect.

Any youngster who can take toys from a rack is moreover ready to return them on the rack. In the event that snares are low enough in a wardrobe for a small kid to reach, he can, when he is three or four years of age, hang up his night robe and set aside his room shoes.

In time he can be given the obligation of balancing coats on holders and placing clean garments in the chest drawers. By the age

of six, each kid ought to take care of taking care of and

taking out the entirety of his dress and toys.

Different responsibilities regarding a small kid under the watchful eye of his room incorporate getting scraps from the floor, day to day exhausting of the waste-bushel, watering plants all alone, hanging up his towel, washing material, and toothbrush, and taking care of his open air play gear.

Youth is none too early to become familiar with the groundworks of abilities expected to keep his room clean. given a residue fabric and told the best way to utilize it, a small kid can rapidly gain proficiency with the engine coordination expected to tidy furnishings. Cleaning toys and little articles is undeniably more troublesome and frequently brings about harm to them on account of the small kid's unfortunate coordination of his finger muscles. Hence, it is shrewd for the mother to tidy the little articles. Then, after the cleaning has been finished, the youngster can set up the little articles back where they should be.

Nothing delights a small kid in excess of his very own toy sweeper which he can use to clear the floor covering while the mother is running the vacuum sweeper. Whenever told the best way to move all light household items aside of the room with the goal that the rug can be cleared and afterward how to supplant the furnishings, even a small kid can do everything except the weighty tidying up of his room. He can utilize the mop to go over the floors where there are no floor coverings or carpets and he can tidy the wood planks and entryways.

Responsibilities In The Home

As well as dealing with his own "things" inside the restrictions of his capacities, each youngster ought to have a few responsibilities regarding portions of the home he imparts to each and every individual from the family. This is essential as the youngster feels the feeling of having a place in his family home on the off chance that he has liability regarding it. Little obligations ought to be appointed to the kid for which he and he alone is dependable. He ought to be told the best way to play out these obligations and afterward ought not out of the ordinary to perform them day to day until he becomes capable in them.

After he becomes capable in the obligations relegated to him, doling out new duties is astute. This not just kills the chance of fatigue with its backup doing the undertaking in a slipshod way however it empowers the small kid to secure new abilities. After he has gained a genuinely enormous collection of abilities, it is a savvy strategy to have all individuals from the family meet something like one time per week and conclude what obligations every relative is to expect for the approaching week. Having some necessary input in what he is to do wipes out the inclination that youngsters frequently foster that their home obligations are a type of drudgery forced on them with no thought of their inclinations.

On the off chance that conceivable, the kid's liabilities in the home ought to be to such an extent that they can be done with other relatives. The more contacts he has with his relatives, the more wonderful the errands will be for him. Besides, working with other relatives will give him the inclination that he is being dealt with more like an adult than like a vulnerable child. Helping with setting and tidying up the table or arranging clothing can all be local area exercises.

At special seasons, there are particularly great open doors for local area exercises in the home. Indeed, even the most youthful child of the family can aid the readiness of exceptional food sources for these special seasons, can help with making and setting the improvements, and can help with tidying up after the festivals are finished.

Psychological Values Of Home Responsibilities

Many guardians feel that the help of a small kid in the normal obligations of the house is even more an obstacle as opposed to an assistance. Valid, the youngster can't tidy too as a grown-up can and he might drop a dish he is drying. Positively anything he wills will be at a much slower rate than the mother's.

Different guardians, particularly moms, may view family errands as such drudgery that they need to save the kid as far as might be feasible. Assuming that they accept that the youngster will be more joyful assuming that he is lighthearted to do however he sees fit, will not request that he assist with the family errands yet they will really rebuke his offers or endeavors to help and demand that he play with his toys.

Such a demeanor militates against the youngster's longing to gain proficiency with the abilities that will end up being valuable and important as he becomes older and it will deny him of the amazing chances to realize when he has a lot of extra energy to rehearse the abilities. Undeniably more serious is the way that denying children ~~childof~~ chances to take part in home liabilities denies them of numerous significant mental qualities such cooperation would give. Which incorporate;

- Sensation of being an undeniable individual from the family.
- Sensation of being grown adequately up to do what other relatives do.
- Discovering that work can be entertaining.
- Pride from accomplishment.
- Cure for weariness, that comes from a lot of play.
- Figuring out how to function in a shared setting.
- Laying out the establishment for helpful play with different youngsters.

Chapter 10

Discipline-good And Bad

To a great many people, discipline implies discipline. However, the standard word references characterize it as preparing in discretion and acquiescence or schooling." It likewise implies preparing molds, fortifications, or consummates. The essential reason for discipline is to show the kid what society expects of him and to rouse him to adjust to social assumptions.

Valid, discipline includes discipline, however discipline isn't entirely there to teach. The instructive angle wherein the kid is prepared to obey is central in the restraining of little youngsters. It isn't coherent, nor is it fair, to anticipate that a youngster should comply until he realizes what is generally anticipated of him.

Components Of Discipline

Great discipline ought to incorporate three discrete and unmistakable, yet firmly interrelated, components. In the first place, training through showing the kid what he ought to or shouldn't do. Second, compensations as applause and endorsement for doing what is generally anticipated of him or if nothing else for attempting to do as such. Third, discipline for deliberate, however, never for accidental bad behavior.

The first and second parts of discipline schooling and rewards ought to be focused on in youth. Not until youth advances and the kid becomes prepared to do adamantly acting mischievously should any extraordinary accentuation be put upon discipline.

Kinds Of Discipline

Starting from the start of the 1900's, there have been extremist changes in what is viewed as great discipline. A few grown-ups, whether guardians or educators, cling to the customary strategy for restraining youngsters, the technique in light of the well-known axiom "Spare the pole and ruin the kid. This strategy is generally alluded to as "tyrant discipline."

In the mid 1920's, the pendulum swung to the contrary limit and discipline was essentially deserted. Affected by the works of Freud and his supporters, and confounding a portion of these compositions. a gathering of instructors supported a program of "moderate training which put solid accentuation on tolerance. This way of thinking of schooling has impacted home discipline and has brought about another kind of discipline known as "tolerant discipline."

As of late, there has been a continuous inclination to create some distance from both of the two limits toward the focal point of the street. In doing as such, the great highlights of both treme techniques for discipline have been kept and the terrible elements disposed of. This has brought about a third kind of discipline "majority rule discipline" - purported in light of the fact that it epitomizes a large number of the standards of popularity based government.

Guardians and educators are a long way from concurring upon the response to the inquiry, "Which is the best sort of discipline for the kid?" Our extraordinary grandparents, all in all, leaned toward the kind being used when they were - tyrant discipline - while individuals from the more youthful age incline toward either lenient or popularity based discipline.

Anything type is utilized, guardians and educators concur that it should be steady, as in it is utilized constantly as opposed to swinging starting with one sort then onto the next. Just when discipline is predictable does the youngster have any idea what is generally anticipated of him and what he, thusly, can anticipate from the disciplinarian. This provides him with a conviction that all is good as well as,

significantly more significant, it gives him a regard
for the disciplinarian.

Teaching For Discipline

Information on good and bad should be procured. It
is similarly unjustifiable to a kid to disregard
showing him good and bad as it is to disregard
showing him how to talk.

Until the youngster is no less than three years of age,
his jargon is restricted to the point that clarifications
of the whys and wherefores of good and awful ways
of behaving are beyond difficult. Consequently, a
couple of very much picked words to portray good
and bad ought to be chosen and utilized continually
regarding the youngster's way of behaving.

At the point when his way of behaving is great, the
words "great," "fine," or "decent" might be related to
it. In time the small kid will discover that his way of
behaving is okay assuming he hears these words.
Similarly, "awful" or "underhanded" can be related
to bad conduct, and "hurt" with risky activities.

At the point when it becomes obvious that the youngster's appreciation is expanding, further clarification ought to be given. At the point when a youngster comprehends the reason why he shouldn't do something he needs to do, he will want to try not to do it than he would have in the event that he thought his folks were simply being mean.

Alerts In Teaching For Discipline

Two alerts ought to be remembered when clarifications are given to a small kid.

To begin with, it is fundamental to recollect consistently the way that restricted a small kid's jargon is. Just basic words that are recognizable to the kid ought to be utilized in the clarifications.

Second, it is important to remember that a small kid's information, similar to his jargon, is excessively restricted for him to have the option to get a handle on the significance of any clarification except if it is brief and basic,

Looks and motions help to make clarifications more significant to the small kid. A grin and a pat of endorsement going with the words "fine" or "great" recount an entire story to him.

Essentially, a scowl, a shaking of the head, limiting the kid's body, keeping down an immature hand that gets into wickedness, a delicate rapping of the fingers with a pencil, or a slight token punishment rapidly lets a small kid know that he is following through with something

that is either underhanded or hurtful. Showings of approaches to getting things done. likewise have an instructive worth in discipline. Every small kid, for instance, appears to be mesmerizingly drawn in by a puddle of water and naturally sprinkle through it. An exhibition of how to skip or move around it will speak to them. They will then, at that point, fail to remember the fun of sprinkling through the puddle for the fun of mirroring the round-the-puddle dance.

Great Instructive Practices In Discipline

Every small kid, regardless of how brilliant they are, advance gradually and forget rapidly. Hence, great preparation is correct and ought to incorporate continuous redundancies. The nearer together in opportunity these reiterations come, the more rapidly the youngster will learn. To ensure that a youngster really knows

has been requested to do or to try not to do From his reiteration from the solicitation, it is feasible to find whether he comprehends what is generally anticipated of him. Further. Also, this strategy assists with concentrating on what is told to him. At last, great discipline ought to be reliable. A small kid should discover that right will be good and bad is off-base regardless of the circumstance and regardless of who is in control. Nothing is more confounding to a kid than the acknowledgment that a specific demonstration is OK one time and culpable at some other point.

Since it requires a small kid investment to what is generally anticipated of him, a decent methodology realize what is generally anticipated of him, it is impor to follow is to request that the kid determine what be tant that he be safeguarded from risk until it is extremely clear that he understands what he should do as well as until he has shown a few times that he recalls what he should do in circumstances where peril is involved.

Award For Good Way Of Behaving

Remunerating your kid can assist with spurring them and support acceptable conduct, and there are a wide range of various ways you can go about it. Not every one of them include giving your youngster material things either, albeit unmistakable rewards certainly have their place as well! Underneath we've assembled a rundown of various ways you can show your kid you value their acceptable conduct, in addition to certain tips on the most proficient

method to make your compensations as successful
as could be expected.

Give Your Youngster Love As A Prize.

Involving friendship as a prize can be a successful
method for telling your kid you endorse their way of
behaving. You might give your kid a high five, a
gesture of congratulations, arm or shoulder, or a
major grin. You can likewise show different types of
warmth, similar to embraces or kisses.
The advantage of involving friendship as a prize is
that it is free and quick, so you can involve it as a
compensation when your kid accomplishes
something great. Showing warmth toward your
youngster can likewise assist them with becoming
accustomed to showing fondness openly and
become familiar with being social and tender with
others.

Spend Extra, Quality Time With Your Youngster.

You can likewise compensate for your kid's acceptable conduct by investing additional energy with your kid. This could be an extra five to ten minutes of perusing time before bed or additional time together after school doing a movement your kid appreciates, for example, playing a specific prepackaged game. Involving quality time as a type of remuneration can likewise permit you to make more grounded social bonds with your kid.

For instance, your kid might very much want to invest energy with you in the kitchen. You may then compensate for their appropriate conduct by permitting them to assist you with setting up a clump of treats or add embellishments to a cake. This will permit you both to get to know each other and make something you can both appreciate.

Reward Your Kid With An Exceptional Trip Or Action.

Perhaps your kid appreciates going to a recreation area close to your home or perhaps your kid can not get a sufficient play zone at the shopping center. In the event that your kid is on acceptable conduct, you might reward them with an exceptional trip to their number one spot or the valuable chance to do a most loved action.

For instance, perhaps your youngster appreciates heading out to the films. You may then compensate for their appropriate conduct by taking them to the most recent film for youngsters, a film date for only you two.

Permit Your Youngster To Invest Energy With Their Companions As A Prize.

Your youngster may likewise answer well to getting extra energy as a prize, where they can spend time with their companions. This is a decent compensation for more established kids, as it will permit your youngster to interface socially with others.

You might establish a point in time limit for this prize, for example, giving your kid an additional one hour of play time at a companion's home or permitting your kid to rest over for one night at a companion's home. Along these lines, you actually have control of the award however your kid is as yet ready to profit from it.

Think About Giving Your Kid Money For A Good Way Of Behaving.

A stipend is a decent choice for kids once they arrive at four or five, as at this age youngsters will generally be more mindful of needs and needs. Giving your youngster a recompense is an effective method for showing your kid the worth of cash and how to be mindful with cash.

You might begin the remittance by giving your kid a limited quantity of cash in view of how old they are, for example, $1 for every year old. Thus, a seven year old would get $7 in stipend. The thought is to give your kid sufficient stipend to get a couple of things they need yet not to an extreme, as you believe your kid should choose what to spend their cash on and to carefully spend it.

Begin by giving your kid genuine money so they can hold the actual cash and figure out how to count it. Then, as they progress in years and hit puberty, you can give them virtual cash, which they can oversee through a stipend App on their telephone or on the PC. When your kid is a young person, they might be prepared to get a remittance through a bank account

.

Discipline For Bad Conduct

All great discipline incorporates discipline for purposeful bad behavior. In the event that discipline is precluded from disciplinary techniques, the kid won't get familiar with the full meaning of wrong way of behaving.

Before discipline is directed, there ought to be distinct and indisputable proof that the youngster's trouble making is deliberate. It is exceptionally uncalled for to rebuff for obliviousness, particularly when a small kid has not a chance of realizing that his way of behaving is off-base except if he has discovered that it is off-base.

Discipline ought to never be given on the grounds that the youngster has been wicked, nonetheless, but since his conduct has been off-base. At the point when a kid is rebuffed on the grounds that he is insidious, the accentuation is put on the youngster, and the outcome is a dour, angry kid.

If, be that as it may, the discipline is given since his way of behaving is devious, the accentuation is put on the way of behaving. The kid's consideration is, moreover, centered around the way of behaving. In this way, by moving accentuation from the youngster to the actual conduct, there is less probability that the kid's disposition will be hurt by hatred.

Unacceptable Types Of Discipline.

There are a wide range of types of discipline that are utilized in the discipline of youngsters. A portion of these are great as in they not just rouse the youngster to attempt to adjust to rules from now on yet they likewise bring about a sound demeanor toward the individual who has caused the discipline for the kid. Different types of discipline are unsuitable - halfway in light of the fact that they don't energize the advancement of inspiration on the youngster's part to adjust to rules from now on and somewhat on the grounds that they lead to horrible mentalities toward the individual who is rebuffed. In the rest of this segment and in the accompanying area are given portrayals of the various types of discipline and a concise assessment of each.

Among the unsuitable types of discipline, coming up next are the most widely recognized;

Spanking : The principal discipline in many families is spanking. The seriousness of the beating is seldom still up in the air by the seriousness of the mischief yet rather by the way the grown-up feels when he manages the discipline. Should the youngster get out of hand when the parent is drained and peevish or when it is humiliating or badly arranged, the punishing is well-suited to be more extreme than the misconduct merits

One can scarcely fault a youngster for fostering an ominous disposition toward discipline and toward all individuals in power while beating is oftentimes utilized. In any case, it puts an excess of accentuation on the kid and too little accentuation on some unacceptable demonstration, which makes certain to prompt negative perspectives.

Then, as well, punishment has minimal instructive worth. Not very many youngsters can tell, after they have been punished, exactly why their way of behaving was off-base. Besides, except if the seriousness of the beating is painstakingly controlled, the youngster will get no hint from this discipline with regards to how wrong his misconduct has been.

Floggings:
The criticisms of beating given above are similarly obvious as to all types of flogging, for example, smacking the face or hands, whipping with a hairbrush, stick, shoe, or lash, or cleaning out the kid's mouth with cleanser for utilizing devious words

Chiding And Annoying:

Chiding and annoying are much of the time utilized by grown-ups who dislike whipping. Like beating, these put a lot of accentuation on the youngster and too little emphasis on his way of behaving. Since nobody wants ~~lakes~~ to be condemned and caused to feel substandard molding makes certain to prompt an angry disposition.

Persistent Admonishing And Survey Of Past Offenses Transform Into Irritating:
The kid who disdains being reprimanded isn't probably going to be well impacted by annoying. He doesn't overlook it yet rather his hatred develops as the irritating proceeds. There is no proof to show that pestering works on a youngster's way of behaving. Logical investigations of rehashed reprimand have plainly shown that the impact is to smother the singular's ability to do what he can do.

Locking Away:
 An outdated strategy for discipline, which is, tragically, still rehearsed in such a large number of families today, of securing an underhanded youngster in a storeroom or dim room. Since there is no connection between the kid's mischief and this

type of discipline for it. This strategy has no instructive worth.

Shipping Off Bed:
Fairly like the method just ~~censored~~ is the act of sending the youngster to bed without his feast. whenever he is mischievous.

Tragically, a small kid's ability for thinking is excessively restricted to empower him to see the connection between his rowdiness and being shipped off bed. In any case, he isn't too youthful to even consider figuring out how to connect bed with discipline and, thus, frequently fosters an obstruction toward hitting the sack. Similarly as serious is the impact of this type of discipline on the youngster's healthful necessities. At the point when he is shipped off bed without his feast, he is being denied the food he wants for solid prosperity. This inclines him toward emotionality which, thus, improves the probability of additional protection from grown-up power and more mischievousness.

Great Types Of Discipline

At the point when it is important to rebuff a kid for tenacious shrewdness and noncompliance, two significant realities ought to be remembered in select-ing the type of discipline to be utilized. In the first place, the discipline ought to be intently sufficient connected with the rowdiness so that even a small kid can't neglect to see the connection between them Second, the discipline ought to go about as an obstacle to additional trouble making of a similar kind with out, simultaneously, stimulating an ominous demeanor on the youngster's part.

Choosing the right discipline isn't so natural as utilizing a stock structure, like hitting, however it will deliver large profits in the better way of behaving for the youngster. The accompanying proposed types of discipline, if accurately directed, ought to be useful in revising misconduct.

Setting things straight. From each point, requiring a youngster to set things straight for his misconduct is the best type of discipline. At the point when a youngster deliberately breaks something that has a place with another kid, he ought to, if conceivable, offer the other kid a selection of his toys or supplant the wrecked toy. For harming another, he ought to be expected to apologize and request pardon.

At the point when a youngster discovers that he should effectively make up for his bad conduct, and that it regularly requires more investment and exertion for the pay than for the first demonstration, he will acknowledge in time that acceptable conduct is simpler than terrible.

The main analysis that can be brought up as to this sort of discipline is that it is some of the time troublesome, spontaneously, to consider a reasonably decent demonstration to make up for the hard demonstration. Assuming that there is by all accounts no related compensatory conduct accessible, the kid can constantly be made to apologize.

SEPARATION:
 Since a small kid's bad conduct most~~much~~ of the time bothers or damages another person, a subsequent decent type of discipline is to deny him of the joy of social contacts until he will apologize and guarantee better conduct from now on. It is by and large more powerful to send a youngster to one

more piece of the room, away from others, than to his own room. While he is within the sight of others, he has a potential chance to acknowledge what he is absent through his own shortcomings.

DENYING THE CHILD OF A TREAT:
One more great type of discipline is to deny a shrewd indignation. child of~~childof~~ an extraordinary treat. This is particularly powerful when there are different youngsters in the family or play bunch who are getting the treat as a prize for good behavior, so that the kid with a stunning open door could see with his own eyes that being great is definitely more favorable than being wicked.

Alerts in the utilization of discipline. Of the three components of training schooling, prizes, and discipline - discipline is the one in particular that is able to bring about negative perspectives. In this manner, it is vital to choose discipline with extraordinary consideration to keep away from, quite far, the foundation of an undesirable demeanor.

Likewise, the discipline chosen should be directed in an unprejudiced, objective way similarly as an appointed authority articulates a sentence on a penalty individual. Never should the kid be allowed to feel that discipline is a type of retribution or a source for grown-up outrage.

Above all the other things, the punisher ought to keep quiet and unruffled regardless of how exasperated the person in question might be. This is significant in light of the fact that it makes the youngster understand that he and he alone is to be faulted.

To guarantee the kid's acknowledgment that the discipline has been merited, it is consistently astute, particularly on account of small kids, to make sense of both when discipline the motivation behind why it is being given

By doing this, there is no way that the youngster will be confused about why he is rebuffed, nor will there be a chance for him to think the discipline was unmerited. Assuming the kid is sincerely upset, it is ideal to hold on until he quiets down prior to assuming control over the matter with him. At last; never permit a youngster to hold onto resentment. He ought not be permitted to have self indulgence or anger of the punisher.

Chapter 11

School Kickoff

School is consistently the principal openness of the kid to what life resembles outside the family and in this segment we will discuss it. As the times of youth attract to a nearby, the opportunity arrives for the kid to go to class. His most memorable school experience might be in a nursery school, in a kindergarten, or in the 1st grade of a primary school. As the law expects that all genuinely and intellectually typical youngsters go to class when they are six years of age, each kid ought to be ready for this new involvement with his life

To every single small kid, going to class implies growing up. They look forward enthusiastically to the day when they will be grown-up to the point of being known as younger students. Kids who have

more established siblings or sisters who head out to
school each day and leave them behind are
particularly anxious to join the positions of younger
students. They need to share the encounters they
hear their family discuss at home.

Importance Of Early School Experiences

Going to class might be a thrilling promotion
adventure or a startling one, contingent on the kid's
groundwork for it. Investigations of kids' mentalities
toward school have uncovered that while most
youngsters enter school with high expectations and
incredible assumptions, excessively numerous kids
become disappointed with school before they
complete the 1st grade.

A few kids figure out how to despise nursery the
everyday schedule, except this is less incessant than
their abhorrence for primary school. The
justification for this is that the break between the
home and the school climate isn't as perfect in

nursery school and kindergarten for what it's worth in 1st grade.

How the kid feels about school relies generally on his initial encounters in school. His excitement to go to class might be smothered if, when he enters school, he finds himself caught off guard for what the school expects of him. Dread and serious insecurities rapidly defeat the joy the youngster had expected.

Similarly however serious as absence of planning seems to be readiness of some unacceptable sort. In their energy to have their youngsters like school, a few guardians paint school in distinctive, ridiculous varieties. The kid who is desolate when his family heads out to school is told, for instance, that he will have a lot of close companions when he goes to class. Valid, there will be a lot of youngsters accessible for him to play with however they probably shouldn't play with him.

Lamentable early encounters at school, whether because of absence of planning or to readiness of some unacceptable sort, are serious in light of the fact that the kid's entire mentality toward school long into the future might be impacted negatively by an off-base beginning. As the days go by, his fear of school might become more grounded and more grounded. In time, he might revolt so passionately against going to class that his folks will find it important to remove him from school.

Going To School - An Adjustment

Going to school is for most kids the primary genuine break with the home climate. This implies a serious acclimation to new individuals, new environmental factors, and new methods of conduct.

To a small kid, whose encounters and common thinking are restricted, any change is troublesome. This is valid for all things being equal slight a change as having a guest in the home or moving to another house.

The capacity to make changes in accordance with new circumstances relies halfway on knowledge.

More significant, be that as it may, are the kid's past encounters in making change. Until the crucial physiological, engine, and social propensities are laid out, the kid's current circumstance ought to be kept as steady and unvaried as conceivable so he can become stuck in a rut

Any slight change is well-suited to disturb the kid under three; yet from that at, vars tions in daily schedule, while perhaps not excessively extraordinary, are mo useful than destructive on the grounds that they assist the kid with making acclimations to changed conditions which, sometime, be wi need to figure out how to do.

Emotional Tension Accompanying Adjustment.

Such change in accordance with new individuals' new circumstances is joined by a specific measure of profound pressure. This is for grown-ups as well concerning small kids. Becoming accustomed to a new position, living in another city or another neighborhood of a similar city, and even changes in accordance with marriage are consistently a burden on a grown-up and call for a specific measure of investment to achieve.

On account of small kids, where the change is more troublesome due to the kid's absence of involvement, the close to home pressure is undeniably more articulated. It shows itself in various ways, the most widely recognized of which are general crabbiness. propensity to cry without satisfactory explanation, loss of craving, hardships in nodding off, heaving, deficiency of weight, discourse disorders,such as stammering, faltering, and slurring.

Preliminary Adjustments Are Helpful.

At the point when youngsters are infants and in any event, when they are babies, guardians will generally change the home and their own advantages to address the issues and needs of the kid. Subsequently, pretty much every youngster gets into the propensity for anticipating that individuals should change in accordance with him.

This, obviously, won't occur when he goes to class. No educator might actually conform to the desires of each and every kid in a study hall nor will different youngsters, acclimated at home to having individuals acclimate to them, change in accordance with the desires of another kid.

The more extended changes are made in the home to the kid, the more well established will be the youngster's assumption that this will happen when he goes to class. To that end fundamental guardians and other relatives give the youngster preparation in making acclimations to them as opposed to anticipating that changes should be made to him.

This implies that one of the main parts of setting up the kid for school is preparing in figuring out how to change in accordance with new circumstances and individuals. Small kids ought to be progressively prepared to simplify themselves especially during the half year time frame before they enter school - to assist with padding the shock that will undoubtedly come when the youngster enters school interestingly.

There are multiple manners by which a youngster can get fundamental involvement with adapting. He might go to a nursery the everyday schedule for a little while before he is prepared to enter 1st grade. Or on the other hand a play gathering of neighborhood kids might be coordinated by moms who alternate in directing the youngsters' play. Participated at Sunday school for a little while previously. Going to class additionally does a lot to prepare for a good school change.

The additional time the youngster needs to figure out how to make changes, the more straightforward it will be for him. Moved preparing in making changes seldom delivers as great outcomes as slow preparation over a more drawn out timeframe.

A mind blowing starter to set up the small kid for his entry into school is for the mother to get to know the school by visiting for a day before she enters her youngster. Cautious perception of the school's daily practice and what is generally anticipated of a youngster will provide the mother with a smart thought of how she should set up her kid to meet the necessities of the school.

Significant Areas Of Adjustment

Meanwhile each school is, somewhat, not quite the same as different schools, there is an adequate number of in like manner in all schools to understand what will be generally anticipated of youngsters when they initially go to class. Of the numerous areas of readiness that each kid will require, the most significant are depicted exhaustively on the accompanying pages.

ACQUIRING ESSENTIAL SKILLS.

To have the option to change effectively to school, a small kid should be free, taking everything into account.

Since nursery schools, kindergartens, and the early levels of primary school dedicate a lot of opportunity to development and play abilities, for example, painting, colored pencil ing, drawing, cutting, earth demonstrating. winding around, throwing and getting balls, working out with rope, jumping, skipping, dashing. moving to music, and singing a lot of time ought to be saved for the improvement of such abilities before the kid goes to class. In the improvement of development abilities, the kid ought to be urged to be unique, not to duplicate others' work or the way things are in a course reading.

Social Adjustment

Going to class presents the small kid issues in friendly change that are different to him. He, right off the bat, should figure out how to coexist with different children~~child~~ of his age, a large portion of whom are finished aliens to him.

Learning How To Serve Others

The defenselessness of the small kid brings about him having more finished for him than he can accomplish for others consequently. Indeed, even as he becomes older and can do things for himself, his folks unreasonably frequently keep on getting things done for him either through propensity or on the grounds that they find it the speediest and simplest way. This results in making the small kid narcissistic, childish, and subordinate. He anticipates that things should be finished for him with next to zero idea of response.

In school he will find a totally different condition winning. Positively no educator will look out for him as his folks have done, nor will his schoolmates. He will before long find that he is supposed to get things done for other people. He will be approached to perform little obligations for the educators and for his colleagues. Moreover, he will be given little responsibilities regarding which he will be considered responsible. It is useful, accordingly, for the kid to have a starter in getting things done for the various individuals from the family and in expecting total powerlessness for specific errands consistently.

Adjustment In Accordance With School Discipline

Numerous small kids are raised in homes where the discipline is remiss and where, sadly, they find that they can do nearly anything they please assuming they set up sufficient quarrel about it. They likewise discover that special cases are regularly made for their misconduct since reprimand or discipline could end up being humiliating to their folks.

Small kids who have had a heedless discipline in the home will find it challenging to conform to school discipline. They will track down that right will be good and bad is off-base. There will be no unique special cases made for them. They will find that they can't do whatever they see fit matter how much fight they make.

Something like a half year yet ideally a year prior to the kid entering school, his folks ought to look at their disciplinary methods in a basic design. This assessment is probably going to show laxities and inconsistencies between their goals of discipline and the techniques they use. Then, sincerely, the guardians ought to teach the childs as he will be focused at school.

INTELLECTUAL ADJUSTMENTS

All school exercises, whether in nursery school, kindergarten, or in the grades, require centralization

9 798840 940532